10

9

8

7

6

5

4

3

2

1

0

Ten Furry
Monsters

A Parents Magazine
Read Aloud Original

Ten Furry Monsters

by Stephanie Calmenson
pictures by Maxie Chambliss

Parents Magazine Press • New York

Library of Congress Cataloging in Publication Data
Calmenson, Stephanie.
  Ten furry monsters.
  Summary: Rhyming text and illustrations introduce the
numbers one through ten by following the antics of ten
monsters.
  [1. Counting-out rhymes.   2. Monsters—Poetry]
I. Chambliss, Maxie, ill. II. Title.
PZ8.3.C13Te 1984 811'.54 84-4998
ISBN 0-8193-1128-6

To my brother, Michael—*S.C.*

From Number Five
to Numbers Three and Four—*M.C.*

Ten furry monsters,
Having monster fun,

Hear their mother calling,
And gather one by one.

"I'm off to buy our lunch now.
I must be on my way.
No one is to wander off.
This is where you stay.

Do not leave the park.
Don't go far to play.
Remember, all my monsters,
This is where you stay."

Ten furry monsters,

Sitting in a line...

One went to hide;
Now there are nine.

Nine furry monsters
Were told that they must wait...

But another went away;
Now there are just eight.

Eight furry monsters,
Up to their old tricks...

Two disappeared;
Now there are six.

Six furry monsters
Really should have tried...

To stay where they were told;
Now there are just five!

Five furry monsters,
Listen to them snore...

One woke up and slipped away;
Now there are just four.

Four furry monsters,
Still where they should be...

Did one forget what mother said?
Now there are just three.

Three furry monsters
Hear an owl call, "Whoo"...

One ran to find it;
Now there are two.

Two furry monsters,
Playing in the sun...

One got up to look for shade;
Now there is just one.

One furry monster
Wants to join the fun...

He goes off with all the rest;
Now there are none...

No furry monsters,
And mother's back again.
"I know you're all here somewhere,
So I will count to ten."

"One, two, three..."

"Four, five, six..."

"Seven, eight, nine..."

"Ten!"

Ten furry monsters
Were not gone for long...

Mother's glad to see them,

Back where they belong!

About the Author

STEPHANIE CALMENSON says
that, just like the monsters in her book,
she and her brother found lots of ways
to have fun without breaking any rules.
"We weren't allowed to play ball in the
house, but we invented a great indoor
game of basketball using rolled up socks
for a ball, and a bent wire hanger
attached to a closet door for a hoop."

Stephanie Calmenson, a former early
childhood teacher, has written many
books for children. She grew up in
Brooklyn, New York, and now lives
in Manhattan.

About the Artist

MAXIE CHAMBLISS grew up in a large family in New Jersey. "With so many running around," she explains, "my dad decided to number us just to keep track. I've been Number Five ever since. It made sense to me that any smart monster mother would have done the same thing."

Maxie Chambliss lives in Massachusetts with her husband and her children, Numbers One and Two.

0

1

2

3

4

5

6

7

8

9

10